GARDENS OF THE UNDERWORLD

GARDENS OF THE UNDERWORLD

illustrated poems inspired by poisonous plants

MEGAN DESROSIERS

HERBAL BONES ART

Gardens of the Underworld. Copyright © 2025 by Megan Desrosiers

All rights reserved. No part of this publication may be reproduced, stored in a retrieval system or transmitted in any form or by any means, electronic, mechanical, photocopying, recording or otherwise without the prior permission of the publisher or in accordance with the provisions of the Copyright, Designs and Patents Act 1988 or under the terms of any license permitting limited copying issued by the Copyright Licensing Angency.

Herbal Bones Art, LLC
herbalbonesart.com

Copyediting by Aaron Lelito
Cover design by Nuno Moreira
Cover and interior illustrations by Megan Desrosiers

A CIP record for this book is available from the Library of Congress Cataloging-in-Publication Data

ISBN-13: 979-8-9929909-2-8

to the ones
who have been feared
misunderstood and overlooked
simply because they were
different

Contents

Preface • 9
Persephone • 11
Skunk Cabbage • 13
Foxglove • 21
Elderberry • 29
Morning Glory • 37
Amanita • 45
Bittersweet Nightshade • 59
Calla Lily • 67
Hollyhock • 75
Holly • 85
Lily of the Valley • 93
Mistletoe • 101
Poison Ivy • 107
Horse Nettle • 119
Brugmansia • 125
Rhododendron • 137
Water Hemlock • 145
Henbane • 151
Monkshood • 157
Yew • 165
Ayahuasca • 175
Ghost Pipe • 185
Snowdrops • 191
Pokeweed • 199
Hellebore • 209
Datura • 217
Belladonna • 225

Acknowledgements • 233
Afterword • 235
About the Poet & Artist • 237

Preface

Humans are collectively undergoing an awakening that is also a reckoning of our disconnect from the land and with non-human beings. Some use shadow work as a part of their awakening. Shadow work has led to increasing interest in poisonous plants and how they can assist us in this work. Those who are drawn to poisonous plants often work with them through routes of ingestion and potentially abusive relationships; however, it is not necessary to ingest them to receive their transformative messages and support. Simply inviting in their energy, as was done to write each of these poems, is a powerful tool to facilitate change.

I did not set out to write these poems; they came to me as I met each plant over the course of several months. Some patiently waited while others aggressively requested space until I took note and wrote down their messages. In listening these plants took me on my own healing journey and helped me to remove the various masks I had been wearing. I believe their messages were meant to be shared so others could remove their own masks and remember how to be in community with the natural world.

Persephone

Holding a torch
in the dark follow me
through and under
and between until we
all come to the water.

Let's float until
we rise again renewed
reborn until the dark
and the light are
One.

Skunk Cabbage

SKUNK CABBAGE

I

Incubate in the darkness
with me,
not hiding,
but quietly heating up,
opening
and rising.

Make the heat
in the dark,
give it a little
shimmy,
a little
shake.

Darkness
is an ending
and
a beginning.

II

Subtly warming,
a slight vibration cascades
through the body,
warming and warming,
hot.

No choice but to expand
and grow, to rise up
rise above the
stagnation, the bitterness
too long held onto.

Vibrating, you rise up
through the muck
and the ooze,
the frozen ground
of your own creation.

You move all
melting past the ice,
heating and rising
up to the aliveness
that is you.

III

It's a bit chilly
        out here,
don't you think?

No matter, we will
heat things up for you.
A little spice is nice
        now and then,
don't you think?

Don't mind the ice,
the cold, the decay
all around, we will wake
everyone up and remind them
        what it means
            to be alive.

IV

See, now doesn't that
          feel nice;
your toes down here
   in the muck
   and the ooze,
  deep in the earth?
Stay here a while
         with us.

See, now doesn't that
          feel nice?
Relax into the cool
ooze, wriggle your toes
we promise we won't
make fun, no really
   wiggle squish
      play.

Play is the ultimate
  form of creation.
You've forgotten how
        to play;
   come back
come back to the muck
the coolness of rebirth
   sink in, sink in.

SKUNK CABBAGE

You humans can be
so silly
sometimes, so pretentious
thinking you are
so much better on two legs,
bipedal, you've forgotten where
you came from, you've forgotten
how to play.

Come back
sink in wriggle
your toes a while
with us.

Foxglove

FOXGLOVE

An aura
enchantment
mystery
mischievous
enticement—

Follow the path
of your heart's desire.
Fairies be here
waiting
for you.

II

There's the portal,
step in
step through.

What do you want?
No, what do you
really want?
We can make it all true.

Do you trust
in us,
in yourself?

The latter is all
you really need;
you can go without
assistance.

Please enter
the portal we want
to join you.

III

So many directions!
Which do you choose?

Certainly not
that one!
It's been traveled
so many, too many
times before and
that's just
not you.

But we three,
which one of us?

You can't follow
four at once,
but maybe you can.
You are your own
unique you so different
from the others
so special.

We know you know
you are one of us.

IV

Joy and illusion
are mixed together here.
It's all an illusion waiting
for you: the joy, the pain
everything
an illusion
of your own making.

You see what you want
you get what you want,
like ink spots your own
interpretation.
Do you choose joy or
continue in your
righteous suffering?

Follow the path
to your heart your knowing
you can heal once
you break down
the illusion of your life
and suffering.

V

Fairies died here.
Oh, you want to hear
happy things?
No, fairies died here.
We are in mourning,
many are forgetting us.
Fairies, when forgotten, die.

When you are no longer
cherished, loved, or seen,
you die, you become
obsolete, invisible
forgotten.

When the memory of you
dies you truly die—
Fairies who were once
here are gone, gone
forgotten and gone.

Believe in fairies.
It's possible to resurrect us,
but it's becoming harder and harder.
Open your hearts to possibility.
Open your hearts and believe.

Elderberry

ELDERBERRY

Drip,

    drip,

hanging

   going

      drip,

         drip

      release,
  drip,
    drip,

            let go.

II

Rising into the mists,
sink into me
your portal.

There is Sun
on the other side.
There is Light,
Light in the mist,
Light in the fog,
Light all around.

You are glowing,
the light is You.

Walk through the mist
like the beacon you are,
the torch in the night,
the flame in the dark.

Move like the mist
move through the mist,
move through us,
move with Us.

Let us move through you,
let us move You.

III

Small but not unseen
each different
each unique

We are stars
starlight and wands
spinning through time
starlight and dreams

We are reality
your reality
if you believe

Each is our own dream
our own star
starlight and
dreams

IV

Do we make you
uneasy?
All these little eyes staring
back at you but it's only one
eye.

Each looking a different
way
but still looking at you
as if to say,
Hello,
will you join us for a while?

Enter the doorway
follow the branching corridor home
we will look out for you
watching for trespassers
maintaining the boundary
while you go

in-
between.

V

Close your eyes
we are always here
now open your eyes
and really
s e e

black as black as black
as night but there is
a glamour here,
hiding the mystery
hiding where you are
going
in the dark
so many tunnels
and passages to follow

but which to choose

see past the glamour,
see past the dark,
see the other side,
the beginning
waiting

VI

You chose me
You're so lucky
I'm so lucky!

Let's see where this goes,
this small doorway into it all.

Why'd you think it was so hard
to choose?
We all lead to
the same place

time to go
follow me!

Morning Glory

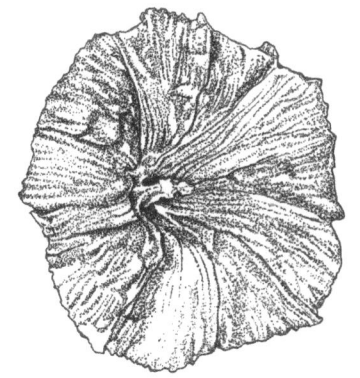

I

dewdrop
morning drop wake up
to me morning sunshine
on your face

delight in the little
the tiny the
divine

soft touch opening
to sunlight
joy

II

Follow the *fuzzy buzzny fuzzy bee* down the hole,
the rabbit hole,
don't get lost,
follow dew drop
follow me

One by one,
by two,
by three,
back to one

Single now
down the hole
to the center,
where you arise
new and whole,
bright and full

Follow me
down the hole
the rabbit hole
to Your Heart's Delight.

III

All closed up
good night,
sweet dreams.
We will rise again,
but for now—
We are rolled up
tightly
in our home
in ourselves
going within

good night

IV

Soft petals,
a slight nod
a bow,
a welcoming,
an invitation
to stay a while,
bask in the sun,
in the light,
soak it up,
dance and bow
nod with me
as we welcome
This New Day.

V

I AM
the portal to your beginning,
the opening to your new day,
the joy in the darkness,
the embrace when there is fear.

Follow me
down the path to
your Knowing,
your Beginning,
the birth of your True Calling,

Your Life.

VI

a candy swirl
a star for you

isn't that what you want,
isn't that what your heart desires?

a sudden change,
a way to be?

all you need
is to swirl with me

twist your head twist
the star twist the heart
then watch

the melt the fade
the puddle is where it starts

the place to find your way
after everything melts away

give it a Swirl stir the Pot
then watch the puddle spin
jump in

Amanita

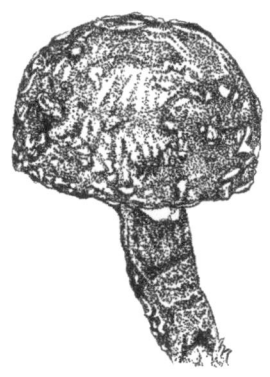

AMANITA

I

oh dont i just look so tasty you know you want
to try me eat me a little nibble is all is needed to
join me join us on a journey down down below
it is completely safe we wouldnt lie dont you trust
us to show all that is waiting to be uncovered
unearthed turned over decayed made new its all
the parts you hide shame you fear

no need to fear embrace all parts for all parts are
you you are not whole without the parts of you
fear shame hide all parts are equal parts that are a
whole a whole you

let us face those parts all parts together come
take a little taste you will see you are whole
and complete your body the in between
the upper and lower the embraced and
feared a little taste is all you can
be all you always are

connect the two the three
the four connect the all
to one and become whole
and put back together
again

are you ready?

it s time to follow
us into the sun the
golden sun it s time
it s time i say not
tomorrow not yesterday
now i say let us to the sun
become the sun
shine it s time
delight i say

III

poky
and bumpy
for your pleasure
and delight a smooth ride
a smooth transition
thats not in order

part of the fun is
to bump and jolt
down the road
down the path
round round round

to the cadence
of your heart
to the rhythm
of your heart
now fast
now slow
slower

ease over the bumps
the transitions
ease into them
ease into me

IV

bright red like a cherry
my sprinkles yummy delight
no harm here pretty colors
i couldnt i wouldnt do harm
eat me it s fun exciting
it s a thrill
it s
time

dive
deep
down
to the depths of the earth
to the depths of your core
it s time to dive to the depths of
you and discover who you are
when you flip inside out

AMANITA

a flying saucer a UFO a flight to the outer reaches
of the universe using you just you as the
vessel to get there close your eyes no
actually leave them open flight
is much more fun that way

it s time to board your one passenger
flight to the beyond to understand the you
here s your ticket a bit weathered and worn
but still shiny and waiting for you

VI

a little for me
a little for you
a little for everyone
candy shining inviting
dripping delight no shame
only Delight the candy
liqueur waiting for you
tasty tasty tasty

round round the merry go
round we go no time to stop
you can if you want
just swing
off you go
over the edge the candy edge
fall down the hole
the rabbit hole

inside outside
round round round
the merry go round we go

VII

Somebody bit me.
Was it you?
It definitely wasn't you.
There's more to taste and try
plenty to go round round
round like a flying saucer!

But first get me in your head;
otherwise I am a dull experience
composting and turning things over.
Don't get me wrong,
composting is interesting.
You never know what will come next;
there's always so much to
decay and rebirth.

You have a few burdens
that I could help with
if only you would let me try.
This process is more fun when done together.
Let us join in your mind;
you never know what will
turn around round round.

AMANITA

VIII

liquid
joy that's what I am
but you are
solid I hear you say I am
liquid
joy your brain
liquid
when you invite me in
a time warp a mind melt
liquid
dripping into the fifth
dimension beyond
liquid
mind melt

how that sounds feels delights
the senses dripping
down
    down
        down

deep
    into the ground
        to the other place
            to the other time

AMANITA

enter
the mind stream flowing
through All Time slipping and dripping
between
your fingers into other worlds
other dimensions but always
between
your fingers can you see it
can you feel the space shift between
your fingers
between your mind where I reside
the drop and shift between

All Things

Bittersweet Nightshade

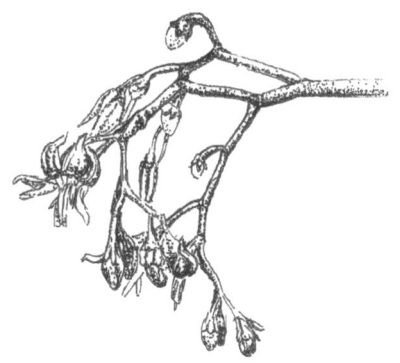

Mesmerizing
deep purple I am
your friend walk
with me through your
troubles and worries
I'll be there
I've always been

Stay with me
sit get lost watch
your troubles fall away
dripping sipping
time slipping through
my leaves

Dripping with
juicy delight caught
in the web of time
dangling care free
perception warps
and shifts

Red the color of blood
your blood my blood
the blood of the ancestors
yours mine ours
blood weaving
through time

Green absolutely green
with envy
not quite ready
hanging waiting
a bit too rigid
to dive in
to melt in
time to go
firm poised

look at them
over there
worth the wait

ripe for the making
ripe for the taking
all colors and stages
present all systems go
ready and waiting

hanging here or is it there?

it's everywhere
across time and space
all at once it's happening
all at once

do you see it?
are you ready?

close your eyes
feel nothing
feel everything

all at once

Am I Death or Life?
I am never sure
they happen
at the same time.

so confusing for you
How do I explain it?
so confusing for me

You lack the ability
to see know feel
the sensations of Life
the sensations of Death
in the very same existence
at the very same time

What is Time?
something I don't understand
something you invented

why?

You can't control Death
You fear not knowing
I understand

Let me show you
how to feel
both Life and Death
not so hard—

is it?

Let go of the need
to understand and know
feel Life and Death
with me

let go

past time
bright red prime
wilting withering
slipping past all time
all knowledge
all things

a pop of juice
a splash of color
and then it's over
and can begin
again

Calla Lily

CALLA LILY

I

slip in me
dark surrounds light
awaits night soft
firm porcelain touch
embrace—

follow my lines dive
golden light rise divine
feminine masculine
light and dark
together forever

II

open to me
ready waiting

sway sensual
dance loosen
your lips ready open
to me close to you
wrapped embrace
colors patterns move
shimmer

close your eyes
dive into you me
one once more

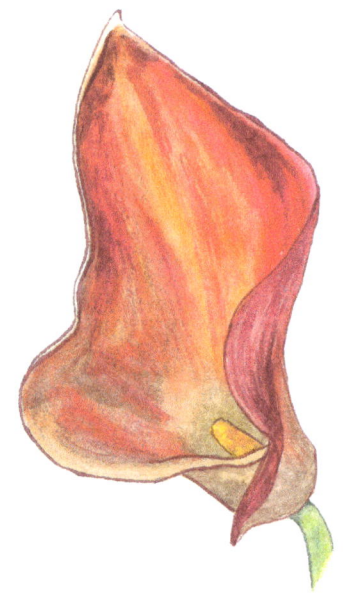

CALLA LILY

III

silky sensual velvet
longing luxuriate slow
gentle slower lick
lips taste essence
divinity

subtle shades soft
shifts fingers
swim hearts desire
bend dip dive deep
eternal embrace

Fading retreating yet alive clinging to hope new life for us now.

CALLA LILY

rigid erect open
balanced firm yet soft
a luxurious state
of being

Hollyhock

I

darkness
the center drowning
light dripping
honey

taste my edges
dive delicately sensually
glide your fingers
into me

slip into center
my center is yours
our center the center
of all light

taste me as we dive
together

forever

II

up down all around
dustings of ice and shadow
cotton candy pillows

soft

magic is the night
shake off within
release let go—

enter
the night journey
below

III

Rubies darker than blood
dark as night remember
light leads guides to center
the darkness waits below.

It's not dark
never could be
the center is brightest
when you can't see.

Follow the silver threads
swirl the hard closed shell
return when ready to
handle me at night.

IV

blooming complete
waiting resting
testing the air
we sleep and dream
of what's to come
what you will do

patience
rest dream fuzzy
sweet dreams
yours deep
in darkness
waiting for you

V

Climb the ladder past
the ceiling the glass
you imagine
up to the stars
where you were
born

where all return
coming and going
life death life again

You are unique
important different
brings change to people
places ideas states
of being

You remember
guide help them
remember too

Fairy dust divine
light and rainbows
not so dark
scary

HOLLYHOCK

it's a dusting off
the magic wand
the pom pom
of delight

reach for the wand
in the portal
don't fall Faeries
don't like to share

they aren't mean
spiteful haven't lost
their way we've lost
ours

tread lightly carefully
when standing near
think wisely before
stepping through

remember
Faeries in secret
nod wave your pom pom
until you return

Holly

I

Dance with light play
with shadow reach up
while below

with a graceful arch bend
lean balanced on your
toes

embrace basking in golden
light while sinking deep

below

II

Red Green
contrast complement
two worlds at once
light dark good evil
same time place

balance exists
at the scale's center
enter the void the cave
decide on balance
in your world

release the known
enter nothing darkness
in-between find balance
perceive light exists
in the dark

HOLLY

lick the drops
from my serrated edges
blood on your ruby lips
the falling snow melts
tastes of salt

IV

Death in one so young
contains fear
to grow shine
in the new day

keeping defenses
too long never
learning how to feel
comfortable in shiny skin.

V

leather cracked and worn
edges tender and brittle
bitter yet resplendent
in glory shininess lingering
past death

clinging to potential
refusing the call
remaining brittle
in the dark decay

life is here
a tough resilience
ability to move grow
shine like a star
on the world

VI

Where
are the snow and promises
dreams of the New Year?

Gone
in sorrowful grief
we've forgotten
to believe in new
reality.

Grief
needed but not
our purpose believe joy
is possible in an aching
world.

Dream
without longing sadness
embody contentedness
to feel the potential of
life.

Lily of the Valley

I

A memory lingering
in the room I smell you
when you're not there
hear you calling my name
softly
quieter each day

p a u s i n g

in anguish
it's too soon
please
don't leave
come back
to me.

II

Bittersweet nostalgia
for a time and place
I can't belong
I'm gone you are gone
our home gone
crumbled
down to the ground
where dust feeds ashes sweet
flowers linger remember us
when all is
gone.

III

Listen to the children
laughing always laughing
beneath the window
out in the garden laughing
playing games chasing
Fairies who dwell there.

Adults aren't allowed
we're too serious imposing
on their small delights
not understanding
the blessing to hear children
laughing until silence
is there.

IV

Little bells
bring the light out
of grief's shadows.

Release the mantle
sadness clinging
on your thick leaves.

Let your tears fall
to the firm ground
shed like rain.

The sun through clouds
brings rainbows
joy that will return.

V

Lost innocence
red blood drips along
my skeleton a mask a shroud
covers the loss
the true grief waits
for remembrance we're merely
blood and bones our flesh
barely holds it in.

Mistletoe

MISTLETOE

You belong up here
with us
since you
used to be a part of us,
us a part of you
worshipper
of life.

Life gives, it takes—
take one of us
to bring life.

Hang from the branches
feel the free air
giving nature
of the world
from here.

II

Snow
silently falling
against vibrant green
dark shrouded stars
shine far away
the ancient rite
through the snow
into the dark
a single candle
leads
the way.

Sacred:
the word meaning
essence of this moment
as all stands still
waits in quiet reverence
as the snow
silently
falls
down.

III

Luminescence
pale waxen moonlight
among the branches
tiny candles lit without
wicks.

The Dead guide
the way from inside
each pale waxen light
shows the way
home.

IV

How did we stray
so far from our
mystical wise ways
and reverence for
beauty?

Reduced to a coy twist
of lips a not so subtle
gesture a quick kiss
dash away.

There's more here:
remember your roots
where you're from
those who passed
through before—

remember
who you are.

Poison Ivy

I

People want to call me sister,
friend change who I am,
give a new label or a redefinition.
Don't soften my meaning—

I am Poison,
one who is easily recognized
I overcome all obstacles
taking down the mightiest giants.
No one stops me.

To be feared?
Maybe it's perspective
I am Poison and all know
my power—
no need to fear.

Boundaries? Silly.
Use me to overcome boundaries,
to persevere and climb, climb, climb!
Careful don't crash down
on the way to the top.

Imagine meeting a wary smile
a hesitant handshake—
Hello, my name is Poison Ivy.
What's yours?

II

Don't you want
to touch soft gentle leaves
rounded flowing reaching
begging to say
hello?

A little color
rouge on the cheeks
goes a long way.
Don't you think?
Come on—

time to Play.

POISON IVY

Do I entice?
I don't mean to
tease,
it's just that I'm rather
lonely over here
winding climbing alone
misunderstood
mistrusted.

I'd like to have more
friends can't help who I am.
You understand maybe
you aren't Poison but are
perhaps misunderstood

lonely.

We have that in common
let's sit on opposite sides
yet meet in the middle.
We can agree on that.

Can't we?

IV

I'm everywhere!
Don't you see? You can't
escape me, we must
live in harmony.

It's easier said than done,
but we have to start somehow.
That's what you humans do,
negotiate and talk.
Whatever words you use,
they have the same meaning.

One is in control,
the other is not.
Negotiate and have
those talks.

You think you know
who's in control?
Maybe you should
think again.

V

I have trouble making friends.
You received my message
loud and clear but perhaps
I came on a bit too strong,
intense. Can we try again,
start over?

Hello, my name is Poison Ivy.
What's yours?

VI

Look at me climbing
weaving in your life
others fear but you
welcome respect.

If you cut me out
you know I know
I'll be back climbing
weaving again.

Let me teach more respect:
to know doesn't mean
to welcome in
your home.

VII

You thought you'd get
away easy not possible
we are bound
to you, you to us.

We have lessons
to learn to teach
each other.

You thought it went
one way we have
plenty to learn from you,
we are ready listening.

Please teach please help
it's lonely being feared,
we want friends respect
is nice hugs are better.

Please help please
help please thank
you.

Horse Nettle

HORSE NETTLE

I

Careful! I bite.
Hard. Not
for the faint of Heart.

You're ready for hard
work the change the molting
that comes with pain
is worth it—

bleed with me let me
bleed while you molt transform
grow become

a sharp Bite
to start. Pain? Yes.
We're ready.
Are you?

II

to dance with me is to walk
the dark side more than edgy
your newfound sharpness
only hinders your way forward
protection is needed while you rest
beautifully held in darkness
so divine you only see light

your guard down while within
my sharp swords protect keep
others out a barrier against harm
release on your return
or be forever trapped defensive
where no light can exist

III

Fingers of Death
tips of each tongue
reach out test the air
wait a bit longer.
Is it safe yet?

Do you believe
poison waits within fear
the dangerous frightening
sleeping beauty you'd become?

In that sleep that dark
night is where your power
and your truth exist guide
protect while you drift
between.

Brugmansia

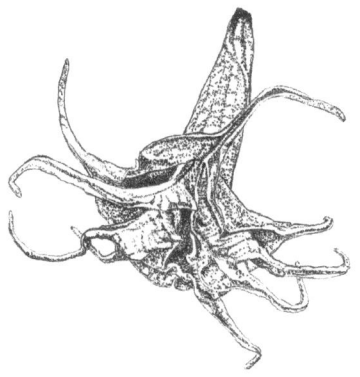

I

Guardian at the gate
a sacred place hush
quiet no noise
only your breath
the forest

become the trees
frogs birds insects
breathe
just breathe become
One

We were here
waiting
waiting
for you a sacred moment
aloneness stillness quiet
entering in dreams.

Hummingbirds were
here too courage
not needed
only trust faith.

Breathe and swing
in the delicate breeze

    *t*o f*r* o
          *t*o fr°

close your eyes
let go.

III

Slowing time
flex and stretch your wings
walk here there
prepare for flight
stretch and flex your wings.

Breathe heaven
nature's perfume
rise high then low
rise meet
that heavenly scent.

Reach the heavens
you are the heavens
speak with angels
you are the angels
breathe float be

that heavenly scent
desire balanced
light and dark
you and me
One.

IV

Death waits
for all no fear
embrace the end
it is light is beginning
is birth is death rebirth
a cycle.

Some die young
some old withered
hold onto love
cherish and share
what will be gone
too soon too young.

I want eternal beauty
remember me
at the end remember
everlasting beauty.

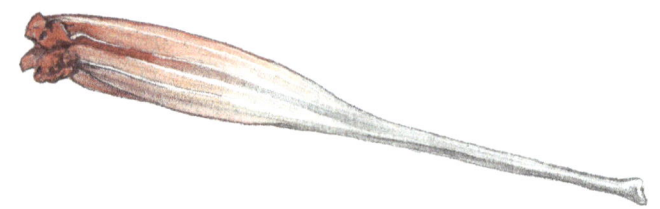

BRUGMANSIA

I see you looking down
at me, I back at you.

We have understanding
commitment belief
in each other.

I believe in you and
now you see my perspective and
through me have fostered
self-belief.

Seeing one another
is a beautiful act,
isn't it?

VI

Growth and potential await
inside, seeds were sown.

Patience as we grow one
by one beautiful fragrant
mystical flowers
created by you.

Don't rush, they will
sprout in time
the beauty unfolding
the journey opening
to your potential.

Sit and wait
with internal eyes
pause breathe enjoy
each unfolding
moment.

You've already
begun.

VII

Come back
drink get lost in me
hang for a while
in the aroma the breeze
glide down from angels
dance across clouds.

Sink down to earth mortal
death to feed worms
your fleshy body
was meant to.

You're ready,
walk among clouds.
Join us.

VIII

Twisting and twirling
the spider reaches
arc here bend there
taste the edges
of wind and time.

Open to the waiting abyss
gently unfurling
something waits
unborn
deep inside.

Waits for you to open
twist unfurl
to the edges
of time.

Don't get lost it's easy
to navigate don't get lost.
Linger with angels
too long and you forget
being human flesh
mortal you forget
to return.

When you join us angels
you are one of us
for all time we like you
wouldn't mind
if you stayed.

We want you to understand
the consequences of lingering
in the clouds too long.

Rhododendron

RHODODENDRON

I

Silent sentry
watching me
protecting brooding quietly
watchful always silent
waiting where the path
begins, the path to future
awakening to knowing
all is quiet waiting
within.

II

Magnetizing I am silent
guardian strength drawing
you into deep
darkness the trance feeling
in your head memories
you can't place—

the silent nostalgia
for what's lost
in space.

III

Soft frills hazy edges,
your edges are hazy too
the blur indistinction
important to the journey
the undertaking.

Haze out those edges
discover what is known
within.

This journey is yours
alone unguided
find the path,
release what you think
you know.

Blur your edges
blur your vision,
that's the way
to your path
and your truth.

IV

One single bud
it's you in here not
out there you're here
reflecting you in me,
me in you.

Why look out there?
Pause, gaze into my bud
it's you waiting
to bloom.

V

Safety waits in darkness
a nest a rest a place
of your own
where no one looks—

a time a place
where you belong
receive support
nurturance guidance
understand your quest
is yours alone.

Release what doesn't belong
go in rest become
your essence your core—
approval waits inside.

Face the scary face yourself
find your path
calling deep inside
discover who you are.

VI

You've waited so long
very long for this moment
it's time to rise to show off
the pizzazz uniqueness
that is you.

Reach to light
heavenly realms
stretch your arms tall
and wide to your highest
parts ready to shine
ready to show
you've found you.

Water Hemlock

I

Mystical beginnings in splits
and roots of my arms.

Some say darkness
warning it is beginning,
we begin in the dark
then we reach far
high to you—

for you are light bright
light we reach to you.

II

stars aligned come
into long darkness
eternal night

III

Lurking by the waterside
warning don't fall slip in
like Ophelia, poor Ophelia.
Don't slip in.

White skirts get heavy pull
you down in dark waters
losing sensation feeling
while your eyes flutter
slow still.

Movements tighten
constrict the cessation
impossible to slow
pause for clarity
a lucid moment—

then sink under
the weight of my skirts
into the depths
below.

Henbane

HENBANE

I

slip into sleep dream
with me dark purple nights
starry skies fly high sink deep
get lost drift in darkness

find the light your light
is yours you can see
in the dark too deep
for others' own lights

shine their lights together
down through darkness
sleep together

in collective death
we decay rot compost grow
into something new
deeply beautiful

seductive darkness awaits
the colors of midnight
are the start of a new day

II

the Twisted tongue curls round
and round to allure
entice you down the path
to your center inner
strength

a Wild ride the flight
high in the sky to seek
what's down below

to find your meaning
you first must know the ground
on which you stand
or you'll never Fly

III

Darkness comes for all
on angel's wings death
wings you can't avoid.

Face yourself the wings
to understand how
to fly.

Monkshood

I

alluring to the little ones
who fit inside where you cannot
open your mind see believe
it's possible to enter be
like the little ones who were big
but now are small enjoying fine
things you cannot

let go leave your big problems
behind bend your mind
believe disbelief
enter the gateway
like the little ones

stay still no movement
not a shiver bend
warp your mind
come in from there you must
from there not from here
perspective isn't physical
it's the mind

II

sunlight
pearlescence luminescence
glow shining from deep
within small drops
leading to center

follow endure the path
lined with the dangers some avoid
you're no fool have wisdom
to navigate warnings

tread sure-footed cross
lines pass through gates
eternal life sunshine
your center awaits

III

star of life or the devil
neither and either are true
both life and death renewal
and endings are there
in me and you

there's potential
when you're ready to discard
what you think you know

clear empty the mind
create become the void
see the other side

IV

when everything turns
brown decay lingering
clinging memory
must be let go

my cap on your head
helps you remember
take a deep breath exhale
release the pressure
you must let go

colors fade impermanent
mortal plane let them go
fade to nothing to earth
feed the breath
that waits

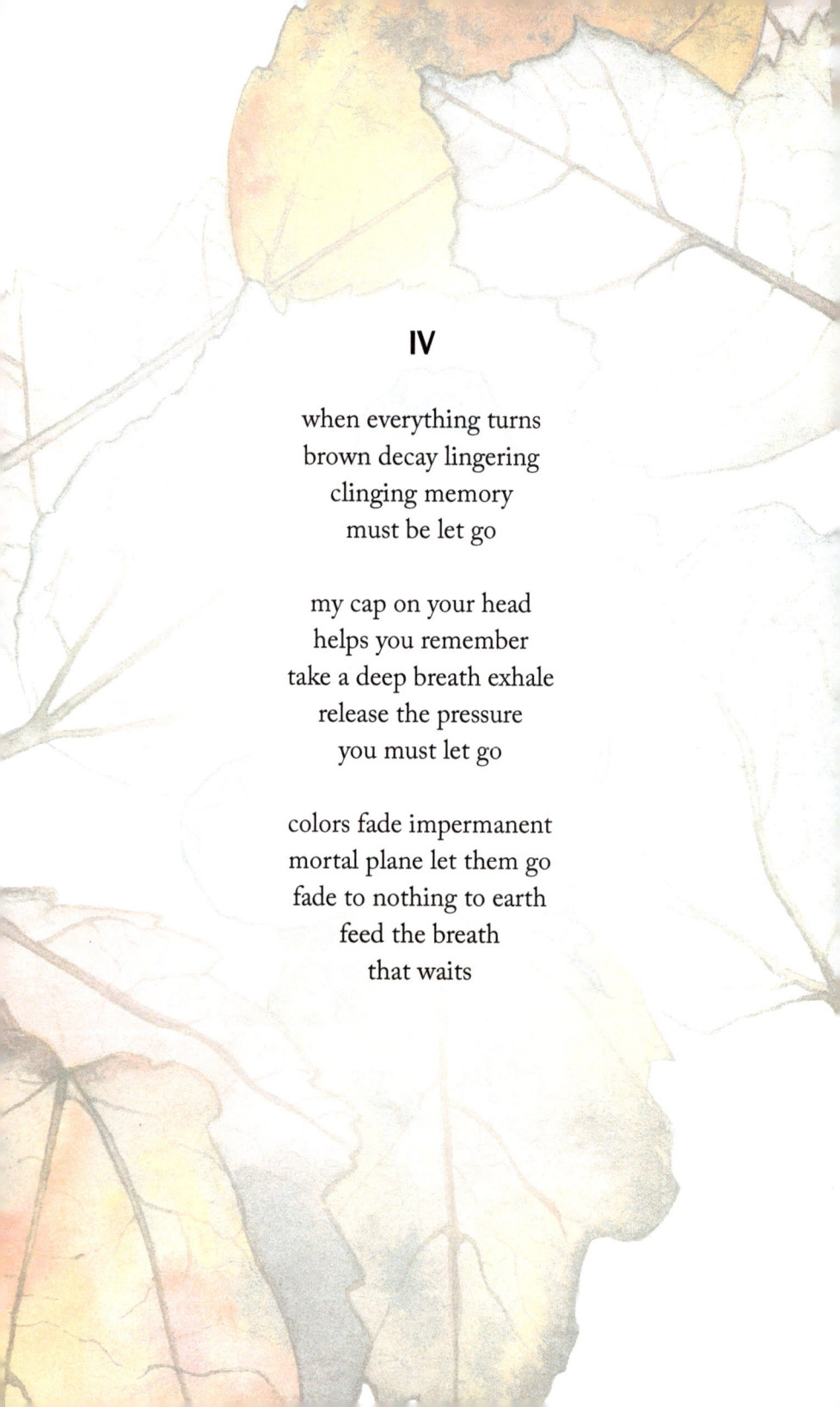

V

high on the mountain
air a bit thin
breathe slow shallow
feel the thread fine tether
to which you hold

release that tether
float above mountains
air quite thin higher
leave the mind it burdens
blocks your way

the skeleton and skull
withering in fading light
retreat become stillness
exposed to elements
time and space transform
your mind

Yew

I

time flowing ripples
each rise and fall
a change a grace
swaying weaving
through lives deaths
transformation
beginning again
as we rise and fall
through the strands
of time

II

Quiet stillness Death endings
close your eyes, hold your breath
see Life a livingness only sensed
with closed eyes, exhale
slightly the moment slips
past your fingers.

Time flows, a waterfall
silent down cliffs constant
change always here there,
pause savor Death.
Renewal begins
when willing.

Exhale, see Life birth
waiting for you.
Step into the river,
into beginning—
step into Life.

III

Life exists with death consumed
by grief you miss opportunity
to see witness your own
new beginning—

life among death may be tiny
small but waiting to grow
bloom larger more beautiful
than before.

IV

Death is there
stay in the dark ending,
it's too bright harsh
out there.

Incubate here rest
go dark deep within
emerge when ready.

V

Reach across the threshold
veil, out to those gone,
reach beyond.

They're not really gone,
there's connection a bridge
a portal to the other side.

Remember the way back
follow the path branch
connecting worlds.

Leave markers if you must
return along that same path
backward so you don't forget
who you met on the other side.

VI

Light on the other side
waits to be seen received
a bathing light of clear joy
renews all who need
deserve healing clear knowing
of their true calling.

VII

A star is born
every moment every day,
as a star dies
every moment every day.

Life and Death
are continual always
embrace the shifting change
the star is your portal,
new life waits within.

Grasp tightly hold that star
watch it burst into all
that was and could be,
all that's in you.

Ayahuasca

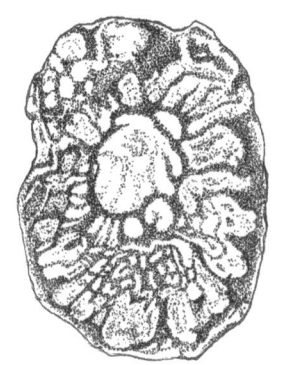

AYAHUASCA

I

The Star People,
their records await open
the door the portal
to other realms
memories endings
beginnings death rebirth
the records of all.

Receiving requires respect
reverence not use abuse,
it's a sacred rite a journey
into the soul to retrieve
the needed healing
to live whole.

II

twisting and turning
the anaconda calls you me all
to long-awaited healing
awakened consciousness
once there now lost
to greed jealousy hate

wake up to potential
humanity integrate heal
become One humans
plants minerals beasts
all beings—

they await
the earth the moon,
the stars wait for us
to come home

III

Grandfather Grandmother
be with me support guide this journey
into the night my soul I've come
to receive the wisdom healing
residing within teach me
how to receive.

IV

I am a delicate flower
fleeting lasting in memory
with brilliant colors treasured
in the heart the sacred vessel
that's locked for many in pain
suffering fear aloneness.

Unlock the heart
use the key of unity
release pain suffering
be free open
your heart
once more.

V

the eyes watch
from the dark no faces
only eyes long lashes and short
look at me silent patient
no words waiting
in the dark pieces break
bit by bit
i remember and grieve
knowing they aren't me
i watch them dissolve

I am free

VI

the Hummingbird says hello
after each journey courage
keep going beautiful healing
integrating

I'm here to guide
your path life
surrounds thriving
pulsing transforming

watch the leaves
open close
each breath of life
in out
expand contract

nothing is still
connect with greenness
fully living breathing
fully alive

they turn and ask
in your stillness why
are you not breathing?
why are you not alive?

AYAHUASCA

VII

the binding anaconda
protects the sacred ancient
wisdom moving in the dark
between stars the void in you
remember to breathe inhale
expand begin again

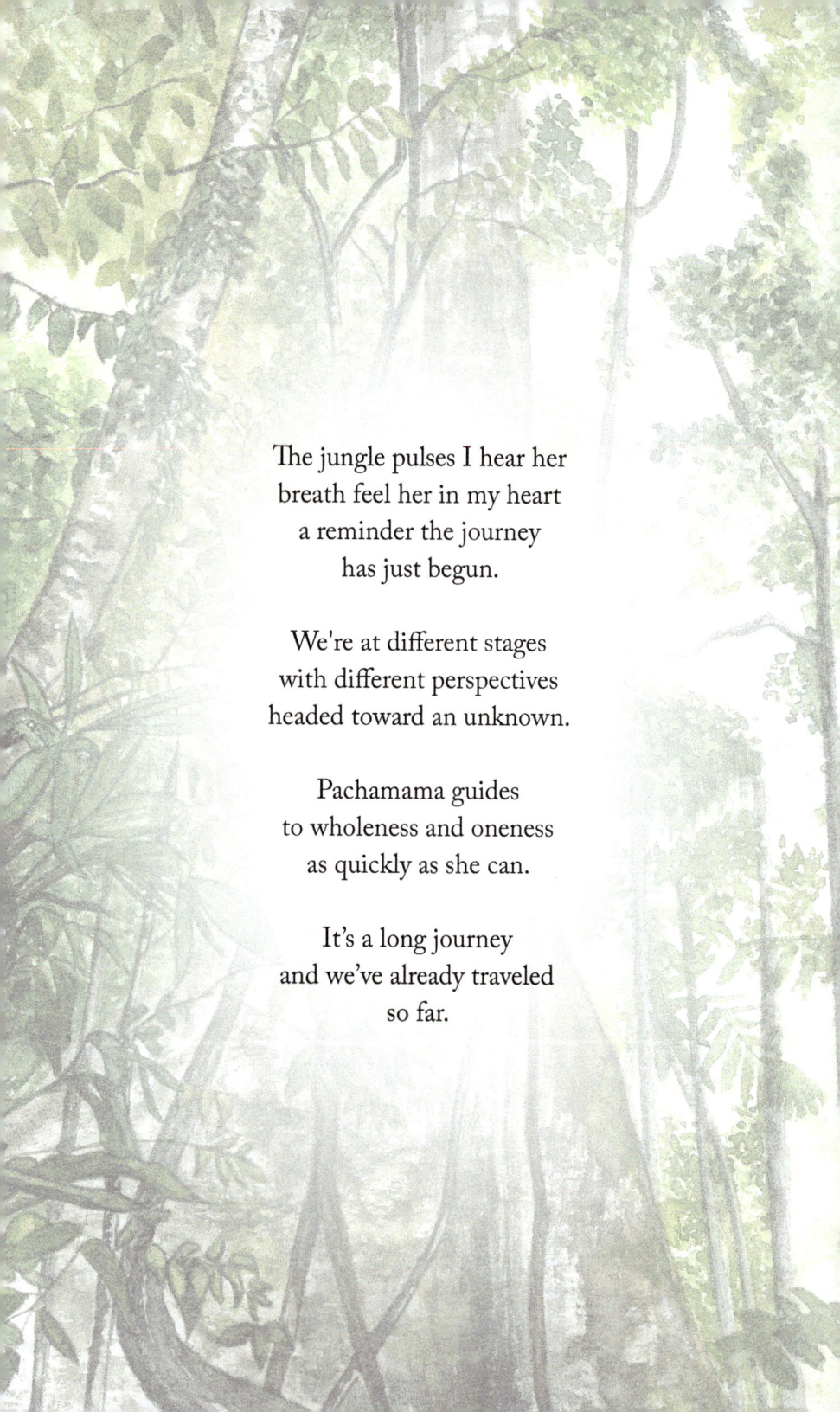

The jungle pulses I hear her
breath feel her in my heart
a reminder the journey
has just begun.

We're at different stages
with different perspectives
headed toward an unknown.

Pachamama guides
to wholeness and oneness
as quickly as she can.

It's a long journey
and we've already traveled
so far.

Ghost Pipe

I

Solitary
no one can see you
blushing in the dark many
wait to join support
and love you.

It's ok to feel invisible lost.
We'll lead the way
as your antennae,
sink into your body.

Follow us.

II

It's not so clear black
and white as you think
you run and hide from
yourself the unacknowledged
pain that waits inside.

Once that pain is held
felt as a part of you again
you reconnect
with yourself,

your depths mystery
you others fear
the truth of being
different yet
the same.

III

silence peace decay
we are that and more

silence peace decay
rising while focused below

silence peace decay
lift above it all

silence peace decay

IV

Waking slowly waking
rising from the Earth
Death reunites you
with what you tried
to lose
yourself.

Wake up to the little
deaths blindly ignored
they rise as one from the dead
wait to greet become
part of you again.

Snowdrops

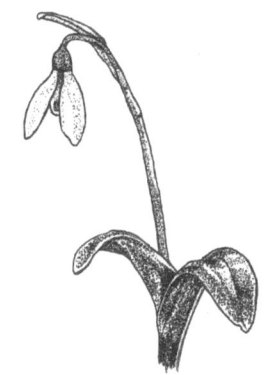

SNOWDROPS

I

white snow reminds
of innocence lost
clinging in cold
bleak darkness
the Winter

bulbs rise gentle
delicate green whispers
the Spring on her mantle
trailing a fresh carpet
of verdant sunlight

she walks past
my window icicles drip
dripping to the ground
below

II

Bathed in sunlight
I belong to the day—

the new dawn begins
a reminder of the cycles
of life and death
dawn bringing warmth
sunset closing darkness.

I rise from winter
brown decay to hearken
awakening spring.

III

Fairies live here
play in the breeze
dance in chill rain
doze in warm sun.

See if you believe
open your eyes to magic
squint tilt your head
just so to remember you
used to know.

They wait down here get
on the ground your hands
knees on your belly
see through their eyes
remember your
visions again.

IV

This short path
is a long path back
to the beginning
of your knowing.

It's been twisted broken
bent over the years
but it's still there
waiting for you.

V

Delicately closed
curled up within gently
swaying waiting
for the moment
of my debut.

Testing the air and waters.
Is it time? Surely it is,
no uncertainty.

Despite the chill
unwelcome feeling
I'm ready don't hesitate
it's time to wake up
the world.

Pokeweed

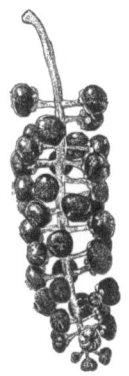

POKEWEED

I

this is where we start there's no end
beginning it's continuum a thread—
do you understand beginning
is the end the in-between
is everything never ending
continuous? continuity not a cycle
no stopping there never is keep going
until you think you're at the end
then realize you're not—there never was
will be an end or beginning
it's all now all always all is all there
can ever be

II

Yummy berries gone
fast you have to be quick
to dine with me,
few remain, inky black

midnight is when we meet
no fear we'll show
the way but it's better
if you show yourself.

enter the dark with us
find the light

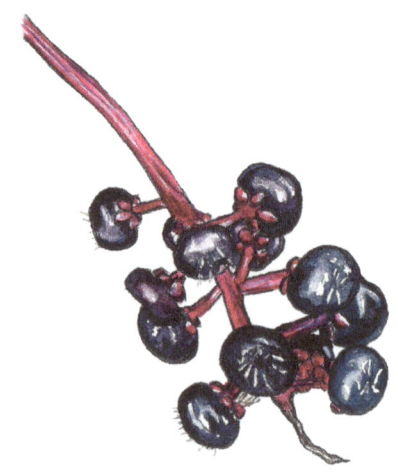

III

connected to the light
and dark we are
the in-between two
in one a duality
you embrace and know

you're like us others
too but they can't see like
you show them how to be
embrace both and One
at once

IV

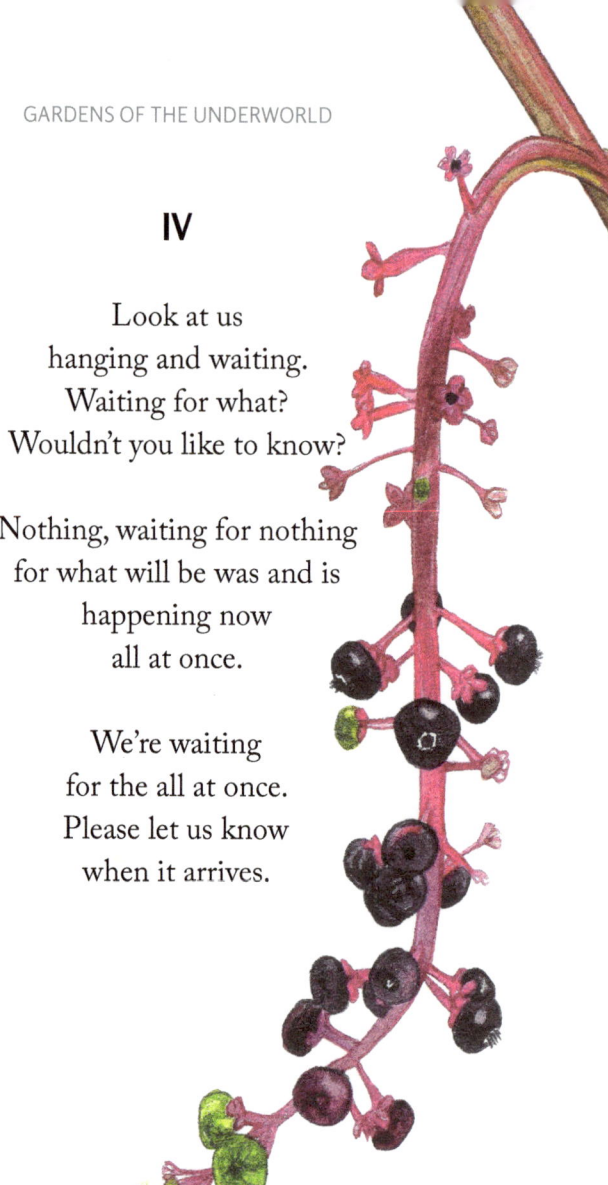

Look at us
hanging and waiting.
Waiting for what?
Wouldn't you like to know?

Nothing, waiting for nothing
for what will be was and is
happening now
all at once.

We're waiting
for the all at once.
Please let us know
when it arrives.

V

simple Beauty bewitches
is a veil for deeper substance
some say darkness
others the light
it's neither and either
it's delicate balance
this simple beauty
is a dance

discover Bewitchment
behind the veil
find the simple
in beauty dance
with us

VI

Gaze into my star reflecting
the magic that is you
glowing brighter each day
time to be the star
and our spotlight

speak for us plants
share our different voices
some lovingly guide
others send mixed messages
and will mislead

we've spent lifetimes
together were worried
you wouldn't find us
this time it took a while
didn't it?

we are grateful to be
found and connected
once more

VII

everything is
ahead or is it behind
it's confusing when you move
opposite grow against
the flow and nature
of others

if we went the same way
there wouldn't be change
you understand when others don't
it's not one or the other
it's both at once
difficult to balance for some

share this gift teach
others to live in both worlds
at once

VIII

It's a mess such a mess
in-between gets confusing
humans make such a mess,
it's simple for us
yet hard for you.

Watch us reach up
down through and out
of this mess we can get
through you can too.

Trust our lead you have to
let go suspend rational
thought to understand
our meaning.

Follow the red line dive
off the end into the abyss
a trust exercise. Do you
trust us?

Dive into the unknown
and you emerge reborn,
in a new society,
in a new way
of being.

Hellebore

HELLEBORE

first
bend and arch up
then turn face down
you must
find the light to reach
the darkest depths
below

serpentine motion indirect lines bend slither come hither you have free will in the cycle circle around the sun with fresh perspective slither round back to the start that isn't the start it's just a step along the way

keep moving
there's nothing to see
only initiates are welcome
and allowed to join us

are you ready
are you an initiate?
we don't think so

circle around once more
then only then will
the door open
for you

circle the sun
unlock the trick door
enter your core
the center

the circle's a trial
a free will game to test
your belief and ability
to find home

like aliens we bloom
when we shouldn't
are sunshine in the snow
on your dark and dreary day

a little brightness
to stand out and facilitate
change with just enough
sweetness to be seen

too much and they will talk
but that soft blush and golden
eye will get your attention
as you stroll by

maybe today is the day
you'll be different
maybe today is the day
you'll be yourself

Evocative.
How dare they?
That's what they say.
Why bloom like that then?

Do you want to stay be
the same? There's an allure
to being different—
I'll bow down
while you decide.

Perhaps it's time
for you to bow
transform open shine
like the sun you
were meant to be.

Datura

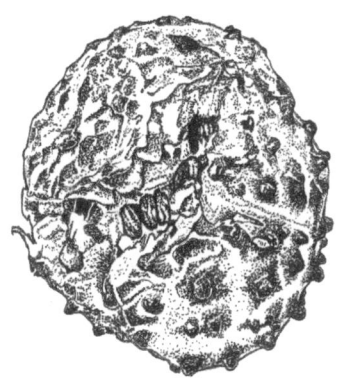

DATURA

I

Growth isn't easy
testing your edges how
others feel those edges.
How do you grow
become when no one is
ready but you?

You test and feel
your surroundings
edge a bit more. Expand
bigger more beautiful
than thought possible
even by you.

Wait with patience
for the moment to unfurl
glorious light that shines
too bright for most
but not for you.

Slowly test
their edges the air
wait for the moment
become the light.

II

You're not the only one
there's more many
are ready to step into
the light their fullest
most beautiful
potential.

Community can
do more than possible
as one become One
join together support
help others find
their light.

III

Trumpets arise
for your announcement
today is the day you shed
fear step into your light.

Leave the dark open
your mind to who you are
awareness to who you were
open each cell to who you can be
when you arise awaken
to who you've always been.

IV

they call me the Devil
how could that be
when I'm surrounded
by beautiful Light

I'm not the devil
names and labels are
misleading a tease
they think

I say—*Come over
I'll change your world
if you sell your soul*—
selling not needed

Open expand into light
Your truest form
awaken your Mind
to its potential

step into the light

V

kissed by a single drop
your Essence I see
who you are
magic starlight—

your truth waits inside
return to essence
to your Core being

shed and distill
fear darkness ask
who You really are

VI

you crave to belong
Embrace belong to yourself
when you find comfort
in your authentic truth
those who belong with
you appear

not all understand
they shy away
in anger hate
they don't can't yet
understand what it means
to come Home

Belladonna

BELLADONNA

I

Starry skies await close
your eyes breathe deep
plunge up into the sky
for up is down, down is up.

You know the way to go
follow the inky night sky
pierced by tiny holes
of light.

Swallow one whole
to join the swoon—dreams
wait for you this night.

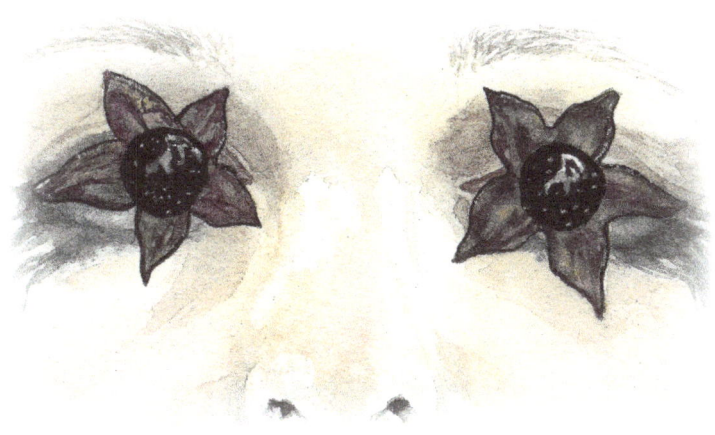

II

Kiss my ruby red lips
so enticing that I want to
a flick of my tongue
and you're under my spell.

It begins with a stirring
deep inside something
you can't remember
who you once were.

Memory rises
from your belly
warms the heart creates
a longing to be satisfied.

Only you can
satisfy your knowing
it comes from
yourself.

III

Moving swaying
serpentine fluid dance
arms outstretched. Are we
touching? I'm not certain.

The full moon watches
overhead I see everyone
despite the dark swaying
dancing closer to animal
our true selves.

IV

While there's risk
in boldness there's no naivete
win the crowd with demure grace
stars shining in your eyes.

Swish your skirts sway
your hips to the rhythm of the night
the morning light is too garish
but oh how this moon lights
your hair reflects the depths
of your eyes.

You know how to move
with grace mystique you know
how to win the crowd kiss
starlight remember moonlight
when you enter the truth
of who you are.

V

Eyes watch wait
to see if you're ready
to dance in the light
embrace who you were
meant to be.

It takes daring
boldness to know when
how to make an entrance,
the time is now the light
shines on centerstage.

Your audience waits.
How will you move?
No time to stumble falter,
it's time for you
to shine.

Acknowledgements

I'm not sure where to begin as this has been a labor of love and my main focus for over two years. It's hard to even comprehend that this project is now as complete as it can be in this moment. Are there other directions I can take it? Sure, but the book you hold in your hands is a place I did not see myself in when Skunk Cabbage first said, "open to me," and began to share some of the poems in *Gardens of the Underworld* back in June 2023. Once I responded with, "yes," these plants began to flood into my life in such a way that it was often hard to keep up with them.

I suppose they thought I had the gift for listening and the patience to share their words. They took me on my own underworld journey of becoming, from non-author to poet and author. I'm honored they chose me as I wouldn't have seen myself as either.

Thank you to each of you, the readers who chose to pick up this book and learn from the voices of each of these plants and their unique personalities. May they continue to support the tending of your underworld gardens long after you close the book.

Thank you to Aaron Lelito, my copyeditor, for understanding the importance and nuances of those unique personalities.

Thank you to Nuno Moreira, my cover designer, for turning my artwork into something I would not have dreamed up; something that truly evokes an underworld garden.

Thank you to Kathryn Solie, whose poisonous plant medicine courses helped guide me home. Meeting the poisonous plants through weekly shamanic journeying in her classes brought me into a sacred partnership with each of these beings.

Thank you to my Ecuador brothers and sisters with whom I sat in sacred ceremony, witnessing, and healing. The Ayahuasca chapter is dedicated to you in honor of our enduring connections.

Thank you to Amanda Nicole, who was the first to read these poems, calling them "gems." She saw their potential and helped show me how to refine and polish them. Without her early encouragement, I'm not sure I would have seen this project through to completion.

Thank you to my two rescues, Merlin and Hazmat, who accompanied me on many walks, often getting me outside on days I otherwise might not have. We met many of these plants along our rambling paths. I know you are enjoying your continued wanderings in the Otherworld, Potato, we miss you.

And, of course, thank you to my husband, Jason, for accompanying me to the open mic nights, and for your encouragement and love! Thank you for your belief in me and for saying that nature is perfect so this book couldn't be any less than so.

Afterword

Sacred (poisonous) plant medicine is for everyone but only when approached with respect and reverence. It is not necessary to ingest the plants to heal. Working with and inviting in their energy can be powerful tools to facilitate change.

Trust in them, invite them in, and trust the great wisdom and teachings they have to offer for you to reach your own state of higher being.

The vast majority of these poems were received simply by sitting with the plant and having a conversation. This was a healing journey for myself, one that is accessible to all who open their awareness and perception to receiving.

GARDENS OF THE UNDERWORLD

About the Poet & Artist

Megan Desrosiers is a writer, artist, and psychopomp who weaves the spiritual with the creative in all of her offerings. Her ancestors call her the Keeper of the Words and she is a contributor to Lucy H. Pearce's *Crow Moon*. Megan lives with her husband and black rescue dogs in New England where regular walks in nature are the source of her inspiration. You are most likely to find her curled up with a book and one of her dogs, wandering outdoors listening to the murmurings of the wild, or exploring the art and writing on headstones in an old New England cemetery.

herbalbonesart.com

www.ingramcontent.com/pod-product-compliance
Lightning Source LLC
Chambersburg PA
CBHW042259090526
44582CB00006B/116